My Quilting Li[fe]

Exploits of a Quilty Cat

By Brannie

with Annette Mira-Bateman

With Thanks to Blackie and Tara

MY QUILTING LIFE: EXPLOITS OF A QUILTY CAT

My Mum's a Quilter.

She sews a lot and needs my help. I don't mind being woken up from a cat-nap when I hear the machine; I know I'm needed. I run into the sewing room, up on her knee and start singing to her. She sort of groans when I arrive - that means she's really glad to see me, I know.

I get lots of pats, but it is a very up and down existence. A bit of sewing, then up she goes to the soft board with the hot, flat thing. I like to sit up on it as soon as she is finished standing there. It's a beaut warm spot to stretch out on. I leave her at least half to work on. That seems fair to me.

From the flat warm board I can jump up higher to shelves with even softer things to sleep on. I have to go up there when she's not looking though, or I get put back on the floor really fast.

The game I like best is when she has lots and lots of little bits and she talks to me (she wouldn't be talking to herself) and puts them all over the floor in patterns. I run then and find my little paper ball for her to throw, but boy, does she get excited when I chase it across the little bits and mess them up. They are good to roll on, too. It is a great game. I know she enjoys it as much as I do; she's very loud at times! I think she enjoys re-arranging all the little bits on the floor.

MY QUILTING LIFE: EXPLOITS OF A QUILTY CAT

I might have to stop now. I can feel a nap-attack coming on.
Hang on! Now she's emptied a big box on the floor and she seems to be making a **tree** in the corner of the room!!

She won't let me climb it yet, but wait - now she's adding shiny stuff and dangly balls and flickering lights! Now she's talking! This looks like the best game yet....

(I'm continuing this from my bed in the laundry. My Mum doesn't want to play with me right now. She got really growly and chased me in here and shut the door......

I might just have a little rest while I'm here. I'll have another go at that tree game later....)

Love Brannie

MY QUILTING LIFE: EXPLOITS OF A QUILTY CAT

I have just discovered a foolproof way to get dinner. I thought I would pass it on to other 'Quilty-cats' to use when all else fails.

My Mum sometimes forgets that it is my dinner time. She doesn't have all that much to do for me - you know, get my food, pat me, play with me, pat me some more, talk to me, pat me again, talk to me, get more food - not much really. So when she gets busy sitting at that little whirring thing that goes ta-ta-ta-ta-tat putting bits of fluffy stuff together, sometimes she forgets my dinner!!

Usually, I just have to go in and enquire nicely and she will hop up and feed me. Occasionally it requires a bit of a smooch on the leg and a tickle with the tail to get her moving, but the other day nothing seemed to work. On and on she went going ta-ta-ta-ta-tat with the whirring thing and I couldn't get her attention.

Finally I did a very big smooch right down her leg and finished with a really hard head butt on her foot. The whirring thing got louder, the ta-ta-ta-tat went real fast and she said "Oh no!!" and jumped up in a flash! Wow that got a reaction!

"You can't DO that!" she yelled, but I HAD, apparently! Not sure what I did, but I think it was pressing hard on her foot that did it. Then she said, "All right, all right. I'll get your food while I am up."

At last, I thought. My Dad will be in for his tea soon and I can't smell any of that coming either. Finally my plate was handed down. "Here you are." she said. "Now eat up, and leave me alone." It's nice to know that food is there. I wasn't really hungry by then, so I went and sat in front of the window

MY QUILTING LIFE: EXPLOITS OF A QUILTY CAT

to look at the birds while I pondered on my success.

Try it on your Mum if she gets carried away with the ta-ta-ta-tat thing and forgets the food. It is all to do with priorities. Let me know if it works. I want to tell you about fur next time.

Love Brannie

MY QUILTING LIFE: EXPLOITS OF A QUILTY CAT

A terrible thing happened to me last week.

My Mum, the quilter, always washes the stuff she makes quilts with in the laundry trough. I am, of course, being Burmese, fascinated by water and I always help out when this job is going on.

Sometimes I can lean over and get a drink out of the tap, but I usually just walk past on the front edge of the trough and sit in my box so I get a closer look.

She had started sloshing around when I arrived. She doesn't always call me to help for some reason; I'm sure she really needs me to supervise.

Anyway, I walked across the front of the trough under her arms to get to my bed. Suddenly I slipped!!! In I went with the wet stuff and the soapy bubbles! It was a bit warm, but I was getting out of there fast. Not as fast as my Mum though!

She grabbed me and held me in the water, kicked the door shut with her foot and then said, "Well you wanted a bath did you?" and the next thing I was getting wet all over! "I didn't want a bath" I yelled, "I'm just interested in the water."

Didn't make any difference. I just got wetter and so did the floor and walls. My Mum, too.

After a lot of struggling, she hauled me out and wrapped me in a towel. Lots of squeezing and rubbing and running around, but the door was shut so I was in big trouble. Round and round we went and then

MY QUILTING LIFE: EXPLOITS OF A QUILTY CAT

she got out a very noisy, hot air thing and proceeded to blast me with that. Wow!

Did I need all that on what had been a quiet day?

Finally she opened the door and I ran for my life. Straight under the bed for a good licking session. I could hear her yelling about "brown fur on everything", but I wasn't coming out until I sorted out the spiky points I had all over.

She combed me later and I discovered that without all the dead fur I was left with the most beautiful soft coat.

I might think about asking for a bath another day. I got more pats afterwards.

Not just now though. I am still a little bit shaky. A good sleep might be called for.

Love Brannie

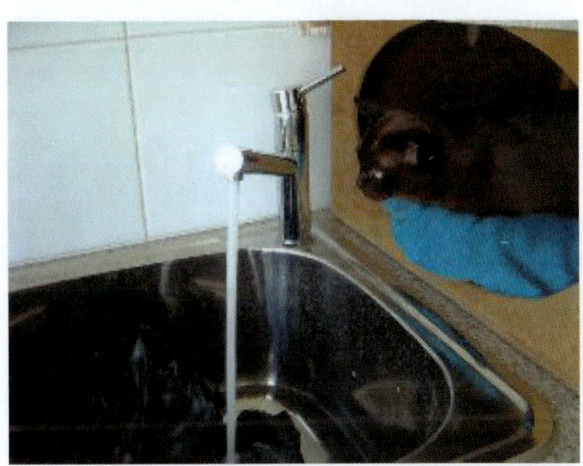

MY QUILTING LIFE: EXPLOITS OF A QUILTY CAT

While the Mum's Away…..

My Mum went to a Quilt Show and Dad and I were on our own for days and days. I still got pats and cuddles, but not as many as when Mum's here.

It is boring without sewing going on, too. Dad does stuff outside that I can't help with. He calls me pet names, like 'Fungus Face'. I know he loves me…

He needs me to sit on his knee when he is in the office though and I quite like looking at the moving pictures, but I've yet to find the mouse he keeps talking about.

Our new house has a big hole cut in the wall between the sewing room and the big-chairs room. If I need a short cut, I can jump up on the back of a chair on one side, then through the wall hole and onto the table with Mum's whirring machine on.

As I am an inside cat, it's a bit of a novelty when wildlife comes in, but the things I like best are flies. I love chasing them. I don't see many, but it's fun leaping around trying to catch them.

The other day a fly flew past and I was off in pursuit! Through the hole in the wall it went with me after it. It landed on the top of the machine. I leapt - chair - table - slapped my feet on the fly…. and the machine tipped over on to the floor! BANG!! I don't know where the fly went, but I tumbled over and fell as well! "Yeowww", I said.

MY QUILTING LIFE: EXPLOITS OF A QUILTY CAT

Dad came running as I picked myself up and did he say, "Oh, poor Brannie. Are you all right?"

Not a bit of it! "Oh, no! Poor, poor machine. I hope it's OK. Oh, dear, oh dear..." etc. Never asked if I was hurt!!

He wouldn't talk to me for the rest of the day, but he did mutter, "I hope your Mum doesn't notice that crack!" as he put me to bed later.

I didn't ever find the fly again. It was all its fault really.

Love Brannie

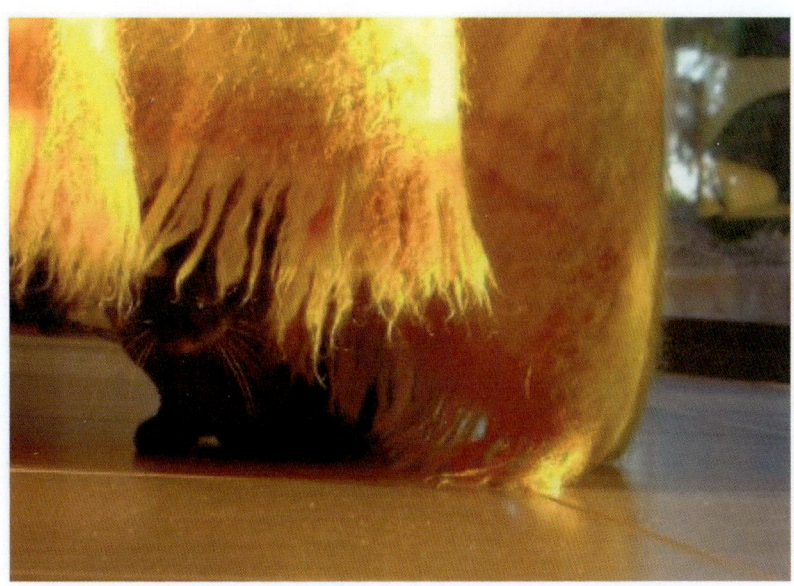

MY QUILTING LIFE: EXPLOITS OF A QUILTY CAT

If your Mum is a quilter like mine, then you probably have quilts all over the place like we do. Mum makes them for me to sleep on.

I especially like a long nap under the starry quilt on the big bed. I spend a lot of time there. Sometimes, when I climb up the side of the bed to get under the quilt, I get it a bit wrong and end up under the doona as well. It's dark and cosy under all that and I sleep very well, but after a while it gets too hot! I can't move and it's sooo hot!! Mum often rescues me. "What are you doing under all that?" she says and lifts them up so I can pour myself out and lie flat out on the floor to recover. Phew! Too hot!

Usually I just crawl under the edge of the quilt, then it's a dim light and not too hot and heavy.

I can spend a lot of time on that bed. I call it "Sleeping Under the Stars."

My Mum and Dad's bed has what she calls a "mystery quilt" on it. I don't know what that means, but it's a very soft bed to roll around on. No mystery at all why I like it to sleep on.

MY QUILTING LIFE: EXPLOITS OF A QUILTY CAT

It is also a good bed to put the brakes on. When I get a bit silly and run like a mad thing from the front door to Mum's bedroom at the other end of the house, I need something to pull me up before I hit the wall.

The soft Mystery Quilt is ideal. (I may have pulled a few threads though, but I don't think she has noticed yet.)

Mum also has a folded rainbow coloured quilt over the arm of the good sofa.

If I try to climb up the side to get under it, we usually both end up in a pile on the floor. That's OK though - I can wriggle right inside for a rest. I call it "sleeping somewhere under the rainbow".

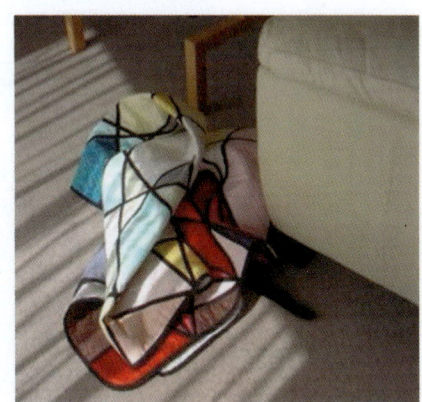

Occasionally Mum or Dad will say, "What's that doing down on the floor?" and pick the quilt up quickly, dumping me out on the floor. A rude awakening!

Speaking of which....it must be time for a little rest on the carpet.....

Love Brannie

MY QUILTING LIFE: EXPLOITS OF A QUILTY CAT

When my Mum and Dad get tired of quilting, we can go for a holiday in our bus. Dad took all the seats out of a big bus and built a table with seats and a bed. There is also a fridge for my food and various things for me to play with.

The first time we went for a big trip, they stopped for the night at a farm a long way from here. I always travel in a harness and sit on a chair under the table. When we stop, they let me off to run around.

The first thing I do is go to the front window to check out the view.

Now you know I am an inside cat with a sheltered existence, so imagine my fright when I jumped up only to find two of the biggest 'dogs' you could imagine, right there looking in the window!! I was stuck! I frizzed up and froze. If I could only keep still they mightn't notice me.

They were chewing and chewing and staring right at me and occasionally one would say, "Mmmmmm."

Were they chewing a cat?? I couldn't move, but gradually they strolled away and with the greatest care and stealth I was able to creep down from the window. Whew!

What were they? Mum laughed at me and took a photo; they didn't seem to realize the danger I was in.

MY QUILTING LIFE: EXPLOITS OF A QUILTY CAT

I have been on many other trips now and I am used to seeing other animals. Last week, there were horses all round us as we had stopped in the middle of a pony club meet. I am very superior to any passing dogs, of course and I can ignore them very disdainfully especially if they bark at me. What silly things they are.

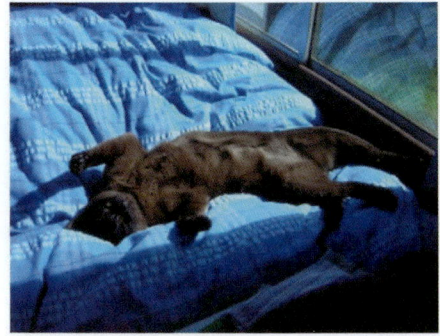

The bed in the bus is very soft although it doesn't have a quilt on it.

Too much dust, I think Mum said. Usually I just enjoy lying around in the sun when we go for holidays. They are always saying something about "brown fur", but you get that.

Today we are doing something called "foundation piecing". It involves a lot of getting up and down and talking to oneself. A new quilt on the way, I guess ....

Love Brannie

MY QUILTING LIFE: EXPLOITS OF A QUILTY CAT

We've just had a Census to fill in, whatever that is. Mum read out the questions and Dad and I answered her.

"How many bedrooms in your residence?" she asked. Dad said "3, or 4 if you count the laundry where Brannie sleeps." I said, "Lots and lots. I can sleep anywhere!"

Mum wrote "3 bedrooms."

Next question: "How many hours of domestic work did the person do last week?"

Mum said, "I wonder if they mean quilting work?" Dad said, "I did full time work doing gardening and maintenance." I said, "Well, I am flat out rearranging the furniture and my toys several times a day. If I run fast enough I can slide the mats around and my tunnel and tent can be turned upside down if I go like mad and what about unpaid 'Quilty' help?" Mum was already writing and I don't think she listened.

Next question: "Did the person look after a child without pay?"

Dad said, "Yes we look after Brannie. Mark that square – 'Looked after a child other than our own.'" Mum marked, No.

Next: "Does the person speak English at home?"

MY QUILTING LIFE: EXPLOITS OF A QUILTY CAT

Well, I thought, I speak Burmese, but they seem to understand me OK. That wasn't a space for that on the form.

Next: "Does the person ever need someone to help with or be with them for self-care activities?"

Yes! Yes! I said. …"help with body movement activities…" That's for sure! Throwing my little toys, playing chasing and boo-ing. Didn't seem to be a space for that answer.

"…help with communication activities…" Well, obviously I can't type this on the computer; Mum has to help there. (I'm still trying to find the mouse she talks about.)

I'll check the answers before the lady calls again. I talked to her through the door when she put it under the mat.

Mum has just finished a new quilt top, so I'm needed to check out how it feels. I'll get back to the census later. I wonder what that paper tastes like?

Love Brannie

MY QUILTING LIFE: EXPLOITS OF A QUILTY CAT

I was all excited yesterday because they told me it was my birthday! I don't know what that means, but my Mum and Dad sang a song to me and that got me **very** interested.

"Hoppy Birdie to You.

Hoppy Birdie to You.

Hoppy Birdie to Yoo-oo.

Hoppy Birdie to You" they sang.

Where? Where? I asked, but no birds were forthcoming. I waited all day. Breakfast and dinner seemed to be the same meat and cat biscuits - not a bird in sight, hopping or otherwise.

Now I am 8. They started talking about changing my food - "for the older cat", they said.

Well, the cheek of it! I can still do the lounge room in 1.2 seconds! Older cat indeed!

There was another word they used. Something like 'geri-cat-ric'. I wonder what that means?

Never mind, that night was my favourite programme on the picture thing. I think they are called 'meerkats'. They aren't really like any cats I know, but they run around a lot and sometimes I can't help myself and I have to jump right up to them to see if I could chase them. Mum says, "Get down! You can't go that close!" They do seem to have a lot of fun. I thought I could join in.

MY QUILTING LIFE: EXPLOITS OF A QUILTY CAT

There are often other animals on the picture thing that I like looking at. Hippos, Mum said, but I thought they looked like big dogs. I don't know about all that water though. Birds are always fluttery and exciting - sometimes hoppy.

Thanks for the pictures from BC and Purdy's Mum. BC obviously knows what to do with quilts and I really like Purdy's free-form wool work. Very artistic Purdy.

Hang on. There's a magpie outside the window. If I'm very careful, I'll be able to sneak right up to him. I'm not sure what I'd do if I caught him.... He'd think all his birthdays had come at once that's for sure!

Love Brannie

MY QUILTING LIFE: EXPLOITS OF A QUILTY CAT

Boy, am I in trouble!

They went off to the Quilt Show and left me here on my own. Uncle Ken came in each day and gave me breakfast and dinner and a few pats and cuddles too, but I had to fill in the time between meals.

I did a lot of sleeping, of course, in, on, or under all the quilts in the house. I played with my toys and ran around a bit. I also slept on the soft chair in the office where my Mum is now. It's a curved chair that feels really comfortable to sleep on.

You know how it is Quilty Cats, when you wake up after a nap and have a big stretch. You kind of stretch your front legs out, then grip with your claws and pull back a bit. You might do that a few times even, before you fold your legs in under again and think about waking up properly.

Well, I must have got a bit carried away. I had a lot of sleeps on that chair while they were away and the back of it is soft, too, so I stretched up there as well.

Now my Dad always cuts my claws short. (He's an expert nail trimmer.) I just relax and let him do it. I almost go to sleep sometimes.

After a few days I noticed that I had left little prickles in the back of the chair. They didn't seem to smooth out again. It's a new textured look, I thought. Oh, well, she'll be right.

MY QUILTING LIFE: EXPLOITS OF A QUILTY CAT

Mum and Dad arrived home late one day and it was all cuddles and "schnookie-poo" and "Did you miss us?" and Dad took me to bed that night; "Come on Bwannie - I'll take you to bed."

The next morning, Mum was off to quilting and Dad said, "I'll just check the emails before we go." That's when it all went horribly wrong.....

'LOOK AT MY CHAIR!!! LOOK WHAT SHE'S DONE TO THE BACK OF IT!!! BLINKIN CAT! I'LL CHOP HER LEGS OFF!!!!!

I had to make myself scarce for the rest of the day. I hope Mum enjoyed the Quilt Show. I haven't been game to ask how it went.

Love Brannie

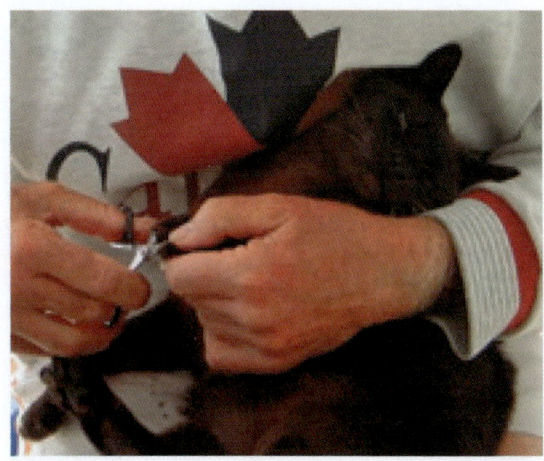

MY QUILTING LIFE: EXPLOITS OF A QUILTY CAT

Now it's getting hotter weather, my Dad spends more time inside watching the picture thing when people play "sports".

I usually help him watch, of course. Mum will do some quiet sewing in her sewing room and I can sit nearby and keep an eye on both of them.

We used to have a very small picture thing and Dad said he "couldn't see the ball" if he sat back in the big chairs, so he moved the upright chairs closer. He likes 'tennis', but I'm not so keen. There isn't enough action; it's just backwards and forwards, backwards and forwards
- a bit boring.

I usually sleep through that.

MY QUILTING LIFE: EXPLOITS OF A QUILTY CAT

There is another game called 'cricket'. I like playing with these things when they come under the doors at night. It is great fun trying to catch them and eat bits before Mum puts them back outside.

Apparently the game has the same name, but there aren't any little black insects flying around in it. Just people in white running and sliding and rolling a ball around.

Quite interesting to me, but my Dad finds it boring after a bit. I think that's what the 'test' is - how long you can sit and watch.

I'll have to watch it a bit longer before I go to check how Mum is going with that quilt.

There might be some pins I can pull out or something....

Love Brannie

MY QUILTING LIFE: EXPLOITS OF A QUILTY CAT

Sometimes I play rough and bite a bit. I'm not a scratcher, mind you, but I can do a sudden hard bite and run. If I don't head for the hills after I bite, I get a smack. That's like lighting the afterburners. I take off like a brown streak.

Anyway, a few days ago, my Mum roughed me up and I bit and ran. She rubbed her thumb and called out nasty names after me.
I laid low for a while, but we were friends again later. I don't hold a grudge.

The next day she complained that her thumb was sore.

Sorer still the day after that.

She said she was unable to sew and was feeling quite sick.

A visit to the doctor was made and a few interesting little pills were produced at meals. Sympathy was called for.

Just as well I'm good at that bit!

MY QUILTING LIFE: EXPLOITS OF A QUILTY CAT

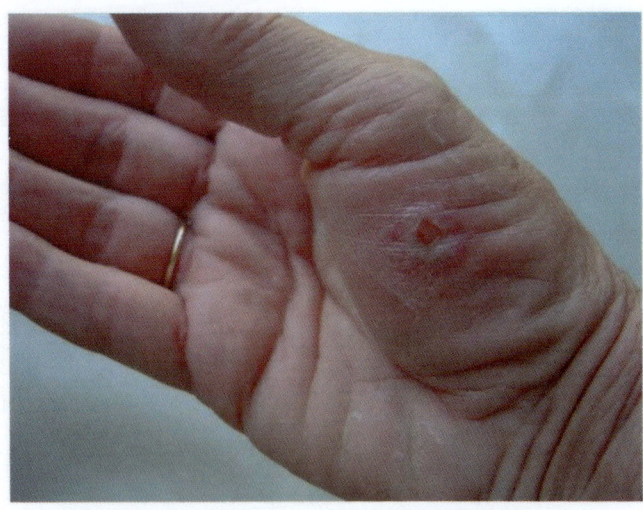

All this time I was feeling quite well, thank you for asking. <u>She's</u> been moping around for days now and complaining that she can't finish those "William Morris blocks" with her sore hand.

Poor, poor sore hand! Sheesh! It was only one little bite.

No-one has asked me how my teeth are. (They're very well thank you, if you're interested.)

Love Brannie

I wanted to discuss toys with other 'Quilty' cats.

I have lots of toys to chase around, but little balls of rolled up paper are as much fun as anything. If I carry these back to the thrower, the game goes on longer, but I can also hit them all over the house by myself for ages.

I have a tent (made by Mum) and a long tunnel lined up with it. I can race the length of the house, fly through the tunnel and into the tent - wham! It slides across the floor or tips right over upside down! Mum may have to make me a new one soon. Somehow the door is torn quite a bit on one side. Don't know how that happened...

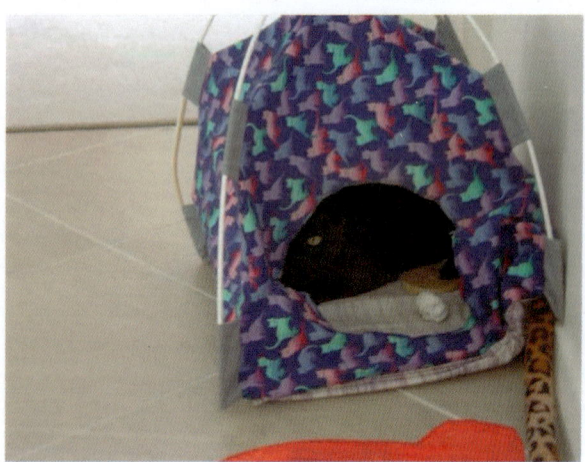

MY QUILTING LIFE: EXPLOITS OF A QUILTY CAT

My favourite chasing toys are the different sized plastic rings from when they open a new jar of food. Off comes the lid, then there is a new ring to bowl over the floor.

I can jump and hit them all over the place and then carry them back to Mum to throw up again. They smell interesting for a while, too.

Dad made me a scratching post which I use a lot. **Never** the furniture – except the office chair. (Shhh! Don't remind them!)

A pair of Mum's old socks rolled up are great thing to chase, too. When they go out and leave me I often move "sockies" to a new place for them to find when they come home.

When my Mum is quilting, she often uses that slippery snake with the marks on. It finishes with '59' in a jagged end that smells very faintly like another cat. The holes in the end match my canine teeth exactly. I think there has been a previous "helper" in this sewing business. (Mum: Has there ever!!)

Love Brannie

MY QUILTING LIFE: EXPLOITS OF A QUILTY CAT

I wanted to tell all you 'Quilty' cats about the cupboards in the new house they built me. There is one in the passage with sliding doors and lots of shelves with soft towels and things on them.

There is one in the corner of the food room, which smells really interesting. There is another one in the quilt room. Sometimes my Mum leaves that sliding door open a bit and then I can jump up into the piles of fabric. I get into a bit of trouble when I'm found there.

"What are you doing in there putting brown fur on everything?"

Whoops! Out fast! Why doesn't she just put brown fabric on the bottom shelf?

The open shelves in the sewing room are good fun. I have just invented a new 'run'. Go like crazy down the passage, a quick U-turn on the quilt room carpet, then back into the sewing room and in 2 leaps, up on to the board with the hot thing and up again almost up to the roof! The final height depends on the speed I've got up to.

I have trouble being quiet about my achievements though.

"Look where I am naoww!!" I call out.

"Get down this instant before you break something!" In strife again, but it's fun!

MY QUILTING LIFE: EXPLOITS OF A QUILTY CAT

There was a problem the other day with the towel place. I heard the door open and I was there in a flash (quietly). I try to dash in and up a shelf or two before I am seen. That worked well (too well) last time. Mum shut the door and left me smirking, very comfortable in the dark.

After quite some time, I realized 3 things: 1) that no-one actually knew where I was; 2) that it was time for dinner; and 3) that I couldn't open the door to get out. My muffled meows were eventually heard when they came looking for me.

I think I will stick to the sewing room shelves in future. Wadding or fabric is just as comfortable as towels really.

Love Brannie

MY QUILTING LIFE: EXPLOITS OF A QUILTY CAT

My Mum and Dad went away for a few days recently. I got to sleep on all the quilts I could find when they weren't there to chase me off.

They had a "close encounter of the furred kind" on their trip, when a big kangaroo decided to jump over the road in front of them. Both car and kangaroo sustained only bruises, but I was very disappointed when they told me they hadn't brought me any home. I eat kangaroo all the time.

I probably haven't told you 'Quilty' cats what good hunters my Mum and Dad are. They go out "shopping" for short trips, (I know it's really hunting though) and come back with pieces of cow, chicken, sheep and kanga for me sometimes. They are really good hunters - and so quick!

I've got my eye on some plump ducks on the lawn right now. You'd think Mum could race out and grab one for dinner, but she's got her head in the "machine" again making a black wall hanging. I thought I would be OK to sit on it, but no, brown fur still shows up on black apparently so I have been given the push again.

I helped her make a lovely bed for my "Blackie" cousin. The little person down there calls it his "nest". I'll get Mum to put the pattern in next time. It's cool and rainy today; I think I will go and get under a quilt for a quick nap - seeing as she hasn't made ME a nest yet!

Love Brannie

PROJECT – Blackie's Cat "Nest"

By Annette Mira-Bateman

Read the pattern through first and refer to the pictures as you go.

Yes – I had to try it out first!

This cat bed started with an idea of a curled up snake, but I quickly decided that if your cat is freaked out by a life-like python, then he's not going to hop in!

It is big enough for a large cat curled up tightly, but you can easily make it larger - even to fit a small dog.

You will need:

Piece of soft fabric measuring 31 x 15½ inches for the base. (We used flannelette.)

A cushion or batting circle with about a 15 inch diameter.

Length of patterned fabric measuring 14 ½ inches x 47½ inches for the side wall

Strips of thick/puffy polyester batting measuring 7 x 47 inches.

To make the base:

Cut 2 circles with a 15½ inch diameter from the soft, cat-print flannelette or other soft fabric.
With right sides together sew a ¼ inch seam around the edge leaving an 8 inch gap open. Turn right sides out and insert a 1 inch thick foam cushion - OR - several layers of thin batting - OR - a circle of 1 inch thick polyester wadding.

Using a fine seam, top sew the opening closed.

To make the side walls:

You will need a suitable-patterned cotton rectangle measuring 14½ x 47½ inches long.

Join the short edges with right sides together, then fold in half lengthwise with right sides out to form the wall of the cat bed.
Sew one long edge to the edge of the padded circle so that the seam allowance is on the inside of the wall.

Insert the batting at this stage and turn the bed inside out before hand-stitching or topstitching by machine the other edge to the circle base. Turn the bed right sides out.

MY QUILTING LIFE: EXPLOITS OF A QUILTY CAT

Stitch with the machine 2 horizontal lines around the wall, 1/3 and 2/3 of the way down. This gives the wall stability.

(To enlarge this bed, just cut bigger circles for the bottom piece and measure the length around the edge to work out the length of the wall rectangle. Make the circle bigger than you think you need.)

When finished, place in a cosy place and show your cat. She'll do the rest!

MY QUILTING LIFE: EXPLOITS OF A QUILTY CAT

I gave my Mum a summary of my day to tell you 'Quilty' cats, but she said it wasn't very interesting and that I should tell you about things I like doing.

I like sitting on or near Mum or Dad when they work - Dad at the computer and Mum sewing. It's easier if I can position myself in the middle of their activities, then I can just keep an eye on both of them without moving. They need my help, you see.

It's best when Mum gets up to placing quilt shapes on the floor. That's really when I am needed to rearrange them, or to bring a toy for her to throw so that I can run through the arrangement. I might come up with a whole new pattern she hadn't thought about!   She calls me ' Mummy's little helper'. Isn't that cute?

Dad needs me to keep his knees warm at the computer. Sometimes there is music or a man talks out of it and it's worth sitting up to watch. Dad can't see the little keys then. That's a help!

They play with me every day so I can run and jump like crazy, but the really BEST thing is when they comb my fur. I was shedding a lot, but now it is colder, I am hanging on to it all.

The comb is a fine-toothed steel one which feels soooooo good! I meow and roll over on the mat for them to comb me all over. It's just wonderful!

They only have to hold the comb up and I run over to the mat and fall over! You should hear me purr! I have the loudest purr - just ask me.

MY QUILTING LIFE: EXPLOITS OF A QUILTY CAT

The summary of my day went like this: Woke up. Ate. Snuck up on a bird. Ran around like a mad thing. Slept. Ate more. Bed.

Now what was wrong with that, I ask you?

Love Brannie

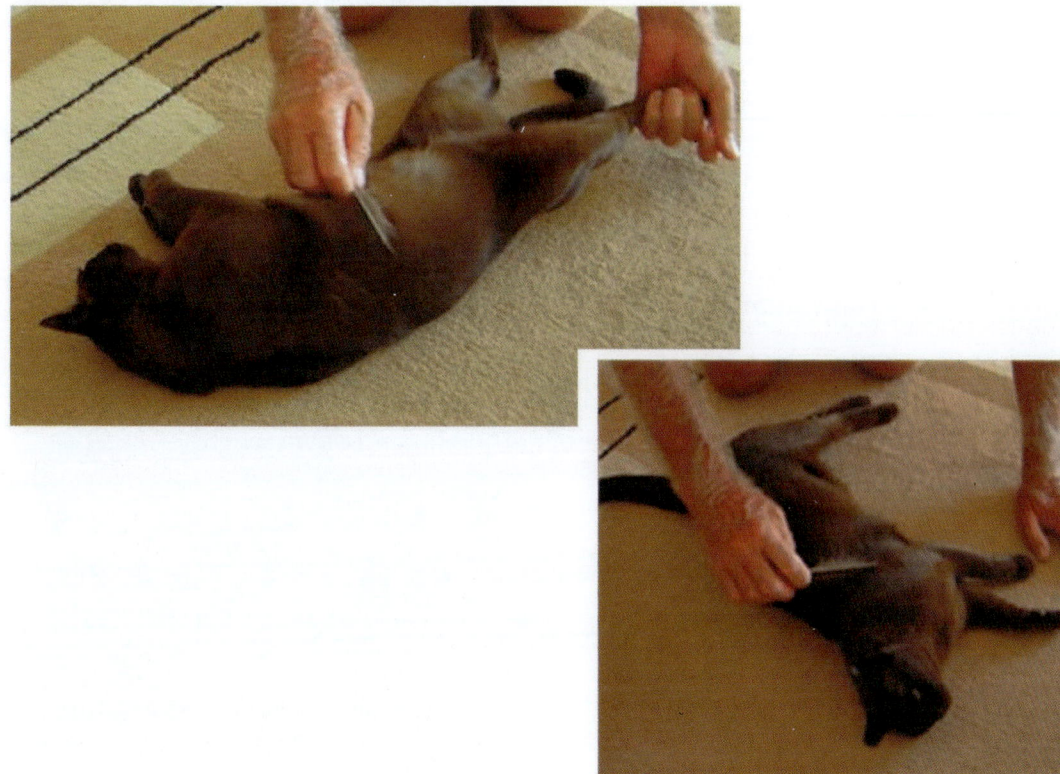

MY QUILTING LIFE: EXPLOITS OF A QUILTY CAT

It wasn't my fault!

After we all have dinner my Mum and Dad sit on the big chairs and look at the picture thing.
I sit on someone's lap - usually Dad's, as he sits still and we can both have a sleep. (Mum says we both snore.)

Anyway, I jumped up on my Dad's knee a few nights ago and the chair went "SPROING!" He pushed me off and quickly stood up.

He turned the chair over, muttered and mumbled a bit, then went to sit on the couch.

"Look what you've done!" he said. "You are too heavy for my chair!" I did a bit of muttering to myself at that stage and went to sit on Mum's lap. She does a lot of getting up and down when sewing; I can't sleep as well there.

Next day my Dad took the chair apart completely. I climbed all over it to try to help. There were lots of funny tools to poke at and I even tried eating what they called 'staples' until they took them away.

I'm glad he was able to put it all back together as I couldn't work it out at all. It was very interesting to climb on and in, but not as comfy as before."

When I did my usual big gallop down the length of the house, I had to do a big jump over the whole pile of chair bits! (I forgot it was there and I am out of control once I start to race.)

MY QUILTING LIFE: EXPLOITS OF A QUILTY CAT

Anyway, it is all fixed now and my Dad has gone out to the big shed to make a box to put the picture thing on. That sounds like a good thing to climb on too.

Come on Dad, get going. I want to try it out.

Love Brannie

MY QUILTING LIFE: EXPLOITS OF A QUILTY CAT

My Mum brought some flowers in the other day. She doesn't do it very often, probably because I eat them if I can.

Anyway, I didn't notice them at first, but when I did I had to get up on the bench in the food room and have a closer look.

"Get down this minute!" she yelled. I swallowed a small piece of leaf and then jumped down.

"You've squared all the leaves off!" she said.

So?

I happen to think they look better that way. I just changed the arrangement a bit. I call it 'licky-bana'.

Pointy leaf ends didn't look as good as squared off ones with small holes and a bit of slobber. It's more natural that way, I think.

I tasted the flowers, (Iris, Mum said), but they weren't nice at all.

Mum has been drawing them, so they might go on a quilt soon. I wonder if she'll do flat ends on the leaves? She's now got the vase sitting in the sink so it can't fall over. I don't think it looks as good in there.

MY QUILTING LIFE: EXPLOITS OF A QUILTY CAT

My cousin, Blackie eats flowers too and readjusts the arrangements - he's usually sick all over the house then - that's 'sicky-bana'.

The other things my Mum brings in to show me are feathers. I'll bet I've smelt and tasted more different birds than you outside 'Quilty' cats. She sticks them in to the top of my scratching post and sometimes I grab one or two and pull them down to snuff at.

They are from a Rainbow Lorikeet, Corella, Tawny Frogmouth, Duck, Crested Pigeon, Mudlark and Magpie.

She's just brought in a really HUGE one and told me it came from an Ibis! Smells peculiar.
Ibis - Iris - whatever. All worth a taste!

Love Brannie

MY QUILTING LIFE: EXPLOITS OF A QUILTY CAT

My Mum makes quilts. My Dad makes wooden things. Mum wanted him to make something called a 'Grandfather Clock', but first he wanted to make a cupboard for the picture thing to go on.

I have been enjoying the picture thing lately. Lots of action from people. Usually I like watching animals racing around, but lately there've been people racing around and chasing each other and even splashing around like mad in water!

I made that ring pattern with my plastic rings too. Mum said I was very clever.

MY QUILTING LIFE: EXPLOITS OF A QUILTY CAT

When Dad had made the picture thing's cupboard, I had to try it out, of course. They put little boxes in the shelves and then I couldn't fit so well.

You should see all the strings in the back!

Meanwhile my Mum decided to take matters into her own hands and she **quilted** her own Grandfather Clock!

MY QUILTING LIFE: EXPLOITS OF A QUILTY CAT

It's really tall and looks great just inside the front door. She says she doesn't know whether to put the mouse on it or not, and that the time is right twice a day anyway. (?!) (I don't understand a lot of what she says.)

I wrote a poem about her though. Here it is:

From Brannie:

My Mummy is a funny one.
She'd quilt and quilt all day.
And when I go to help her sew,
She says I'm in the way!

I always test the quilts out,
But I shed a bit of fur.
Then when she yells at me to go
I roll and purr and purr.

MY QUILTING LIFE: EXPLOITS OF A QUILTY CAT

She makes up quilts called 'colour wash'
Lays pieces on the floor.
And when I race right through them
There's little bits galore!

I chase round after cotton reels;
I really love to play.
But when I make the cotton fly
She says I'm in the way!
She sews a lot by hand as well;
And I know that she loves me.
As soon as she threads that needle up
She invites me to her nice warm knee.

So now I'm throwing cotton reels-
I'm batting them away.
Oh No! They've gone under her chair!
Now she's got in MY way!

Love Brannie

MY QUILTING LIFE: EXPLOITS OF A QUILTY CAT

The other day my Mum and Dad went out what they call 'shopping', but I know it was hunting because they came back with fresh meat for me.

My Dad likes to cook and before they left, he had made some muffins. They left them on a rack high up in the food room. It smelt really good so I got up to have a look.

I had a little lick at one to check on the taste. Quite nice really! I licked a bit more. After a while I got to the bits of gooey soft stuff which didn't taste as good, so I got down and had a nap on the bed.

When they arrived home and went into the food room with their bags and parcels it was all - "WHO'S BEEN EATING MY MUFFINS? BY GOLLY, YOU'RE IN TROUBLE, CAT!!

Talk about an over-reaction! I only tried **one** of them, after all! Then he remembered it will be my birthday in a short time, so he said, "No birthday cake for you, Miss! You've had it early."
I could hear him muttering that I only stopped at the strawberries or mulberries, or I would have eaten the whole lot!

He threatened to send me off with Mum to her Quilting Retreat this weekend. The ladies would probably be nice to me. I am an expert at helping to quilt after all. Think of all the quilts I could test out. I wonder if they would have muffins for morning tea?

MY QUILTING LIFE: EXPLOITS OF A QUILTY CAT

I'm not sure how to tactfully suggest that Dad leaves out the strawberries and mulberries next time. Any ideas 'Quilty' cats?

Love Brannie

MY QUILTING LIFE: EXPLOITS OF A QUILTY CAT

My Mum went to the Quilt Show. She was away for days and days. Dad and I were on our own. I tried to pack myself in her bag, but she kept putting me out. I knew she wouldn't need a jumper (sweater) and could have fitted me instead.

My Dad even complained about me when he talked to her on the phone. "That darn cat! Every time I sit down, she's on my knee! She even calls out to me when I go out to the shed." Well, of course. I was missing a lot of pats and 'knee time' with my Mum.

My Dad does different shopping when Mum's away. We eat creamy ice cream and try out different cakes, especially ones with lots of chocolate in. He also bought me a new box of nunkies. (You know, those little cat biscuits - we call them nunkies.)

I could smell something very interesting in the food room and it took me a while to find the box on the floor of the food cupboard. It had a very handsome blue Burmese boy on the front of the box; I spent quite a bit of time sitting beside him in the dark sniffing the wonderful smells of new nunkies.

When my Dad opened the box, however, although the picture of the hunky blue chap remained as tasty, the nunkies weren't as I expected - not as nice as the ones before. What a disappointment! My Mum calls it 'deceptive packaging'. I call it a real shame. It's a big box of nunkies I have to get through!

Anyway, here's the recipe for those Muffins I ate last time. (Other 'Quilty' cats would probably prefer it if you left out the berries. My Mum and Dad liked them in.)

Mulberry White Chocolate Muffins
* 2 ¼ cups self-raising flour (or All purpose flour + 1 tspn baking powder)
* 1 ½ cups fresh berries, grated apple or chopped fruit
* ¼ cup white chocolate bits or nuts
* 240 ml (1 cup) buttermilk
* 2 eggs
* 80 ml (1/3 cup) canola oil
* ¾ cup sugar
* 1 teaspoon vanilla essence

Pre-heat oven to 200 deg.C (400 deg. F). Either grease muffin pans or line with baking paper or muffin cases to prevent sticking.

Whisk all wet ingredients together. Gently fold in flour until almost incorporated. Fold in chocolate or nuts, berries or fruit.

Bake for 8 minutes at 200 deg. C (400 deg F) then turn oven down to 170 deg.C (340 deg F) for a further 15 to 25 minutes depending on the size of the muffins.

Allow to sit in the pan for 5 minutes before turning out. Serve warm, or freeze and zap in the oven or microwave.

Love Brannie

Something's going on in our house. I think some of those little people are coming for a visit soon. Mum keeps talking about "getting the tree out again".

Now, I seem to remember a long time ago helping her build a tree inside. I got into trouble for climbing it and swinging on things. I thought that's what it was for!

She's also been using valuable sewing time doing other things. Like helping Dad dig big holes outside and then filling them in again with stuff my Dad mixes in the wheeling thing. I don't see the point in it at all. They have built a wall and they talk about a roof.

The trouble is they come in all hot and sweaty, drink heaps of water then just groan and flop in a chair.

I have great trouble getting them to play with me. "We're tired", they say. "We've been working hard!"

Well! I've been looking out at them digging. It's hard work just staying awake sometimes, but usually work fascinates me; I could watch it for hours.

MY QUILTING LIFE: EXPLOITS OF A QUILTY CAT

My Mum has also been busy wrapping things in paper. There's stringy stuff involved as well. Great fun! Parcels are appearing and I've been warned not to even <u>think</u> about chewing on anything.

I'll have to go now. My Dad has just carried a big length of something past the window. I need to watch to make sure it is going in the right place.

Mum wrote a poem called "Help!" What does that little line after the word mean?

"<u>Help</u>!"
What a wonderful thing making quilts is!
With patterns and pieces and stitches.
If you're thinking a cat
Could be helpful with that,
Well you know how much help a Burmese is!

Love Brannie

MY QUILTING LIFE: EXPLOITS OF A QUILTY CAT

My Dad looked up Burmese cats on the computer. I discovered quite a lot about my ancestors.

Apparently.....we're all descended from "an imported female called Wong Mau". Now visitors have often said that I had a funny meow, but I don't think there is anything wong with it. All us Burmese cats have deep voices which we like to use frequently.

The computer says we're "very vocal and often call their owners". Well, of course! Mum and I chat all the time - when I'm awake that is.

She needs to talk to me to get all those quilt measurements right, just like I need to walk all over everything and enquire if she needs any help.

She's been talking about a "Baltimore" design lately, whatever that is.

It involves cutting up paper into big squares and then drawing things on them. Then saying, "No, I don't like that one. What about more flowers or different leaves?"

I offer assistance by -

(a) sitting on the pile of paper squares;
(b) chewing a few corners;
(c) running through the sheets on the floor to scatter them or
(d) all of the above and then going to bed for a quick nap.

MY QUILTING LIFE: EXPLOITS OF A QUILTY CAT

She's got out that tree I was telling you about last time. I've been very good and not tried to climb or chew it, but I discovered the box it came in is really good fun! Great for boo-ing games.

I hope all you other 'Quilty' cats had fun at this time of the year. I enjoyed trying some of the different animals they talked about. Things called turkeys and prawns sound a bit all right!

Just have to figure out now how to my paws on more....

Must go. I'm going to try meowing loudly in that tree box to see how that sounds. Not wong, that's for sure.

Love Brannie

MY QUILTING LIFE: EXPLOITS OF A QUILTY CAT

It's been really hot here lately and I didn't get much sleep last night. They'd just put me to bed in the laundry and shut me in when the flash-bang storm arrived. I'm not very keen on them, so I asked nicely, "Can I come out please?", but they only called out, "You're all right. It's only Funder."

After the next couple of crashes shook the house, I yelled out **"I want to come out NAOW!"**

Then they let me out, gave me cuddles and said, "It's quite OK. Won't hurt you. Just Funder."

Well it didn't sound like Fun to me!! They didn't seem to be having much fun either! They raced around shutting windows and switching things off and saying things like "Whoa, look out!" and "That was close!" (You're telling me it was close! I didn't think they would appreciate me asking if they were having any Fun yet.)

So I stayed out and slept on the corner of Mum's bed. It was quite a hot night. I slept at her feet; I slept beside her legs; I slept under her arm(s). I walked up her a couple of times to see if she was asleep. I'd usually get a pat - and a groan.

The Funder faded away eventually and finally it got light again. Now today, Mum says she is too tired to quilt and it is really too hot as well.

MY QUILTING LIFE: EXPLOITS OF A QUILTY CAT

We've all had a nap-attack this afternoon which suited me just fine. I was quite sleepy after my busy night.

I hope more Funder doesn't come tonight; it really wasn't much fun at all. I wonder why they call it that?

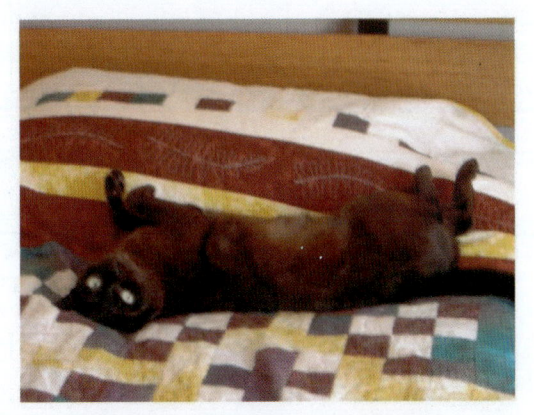

(Me recovering after a busy night)

Love Brannie

MY QUILTING LIFE: EXPLOITS OF A QUILTY CAT

My Quilty Mum and Dad went away to visit those little people again and left me with Uncle Ken.

He fed me, but didn't give me as many pats and cuddles as I'm used to. I was so-o-o pleased to have them back. I've done a lot of smooching and purring, but I am a bit sick of hearing about "Robbie".

Apparently Auntie Jody has a small rabbit called "Robbie".

Now, my Mum calls <u>me</u> "Bunny" quite a lot - I'm sure it means she loves me.

As in: "Hello Brannie-bunny. Have you been having a nice sleep?"

or "Here comes the Bunny-Cat. Didn't you know I was sewing and needed help?"

Now it's Robbie this and Robbie that. I'd like to meet him. He sounds delicious!

There are a few bunnies outside here that I'd like to catch, too. I want to be the only "Bunny" in this house though. There was even a song on the music thing about rabbits. It went on and on about "Bunny, bunny, bunny..." Sheesh! Too much altogether!

I think I will curl up on the batting pile for a while. Mum is talking to herself and sewing little bits together again. She can do without my help for a bit.

Apparently it's going to be a 'table runner'. I'm a pretty good floor runner, but she can't mean what that sounds like. I'll wait and see.

MY QUILTING LIFE: EXPLOITS OF A QUILTY CAT

(She's still muttering about rabbits. Now it's one with a funny name - "Easter". Perhaps if I have a nap, they'll all go away.)

Love Brannie

MY QUILTING LIFE: EXPLOITS OF A QUILTY CAT

I've had a sore leg. My Dad thinks it's something to do with Arthur-something-something, but I don't know anyone called Arthur.

I think I hurt my shoulder when I crashed into the lounge room wall. Sometimes I run so fast, I can't turn in time to complete the circuit. Anyway I have been limping around for a while. (I get more cuddles, I've discovered.)

My 'Quilty' Mum has been trimming long skinny bits off big dark squares she's cut out.

She tied several of them together and hung them on the door handle next to where she was cutting.

I was then able to do summersaults and jumps with the skinny bits while she worked and talked to me.

I really don't know what she'd do without me to help. All the jumping and rolling around didn't do my leg much good though.

MY QUILTING LIFE: EXPLOITS OF A QUILTY CAT

That night they put my bed-box on the floor in the laundry. It is always up on the bench. They said it was to save me jumping up, but it was all wrong! I couldn't sleep facing the wrong way! I called out all night.

"My box is <u>dowwwn</u> on the floor!" "I want to get <u>owwwt</u>!" "I can't sleep <u>naoww</u>!"

I was **so** tired the next day - I hadn't slept a wink all night!

I noticed Mum was a bit staggery and bleary-eyed when she let me out in the morning. Don't know what was wrong with **her!** I had to sleep all day to catch up! I didn't stir the next night - safely up on the bench again.

She's been doing some knitting as well. Now that is something I am really expert at.

You can sleep on the knee and reach out every now and then to hook a bit of wool on the way past.

The bits she's finished have lots of dingly dangle bits hanging on them too. Knitting is good fun and not as strenuous as quilting.

It's quite restful for sore legs…

Love Brannie

MY QUILTING LIFE: EXPLOITS OF A QUILTY CAT

When my Mum put me to bed a few sleeps ago, she said I could have a "sleep in" because we were going to "save daylight".

I got thinking about that in the night and decided I could save daylight best by waking up early.

So I started calling out early for someone to get me out. It took ages, but Mum finally came and opened the door, and I purred loudly, expecting thanks.

"YOU CAN'T SAVE DAYLIGHT AT 3 A.M.!!!!" she yelled.

I was so sure I was helping. Of course once she had let the cat out of the bag (so to speak), there was no going back and I got to spend the rest of the night on the bed. And then they didn't get up until late!
I thought breakfast was never coming. Don't tell me they are trying to "save breakfast" next!

Actually Mum has been putting fishy-tasting oily stuff on my meat. I don't mind it now, but it was yukky at first.
My sore leg is quite good again now, by the way. I am back to playing silly-devils again anyway.

Hey. I've got to go. It's cuppa time and they might give me some of that Banana Cake my Dad makes. It's really yummy, but go easy on the chocolate. I'll get Mum to put the recipe in.

Some serious smooching coming up - and staring helps too...

Brannie's Banana Bread

8 tablespoons caster sugar

370g (or about 3 medium) ripe bananas

1/2 cup vegetable oil

2 eggs

270g (10 or 11 ozs.) self-raising flour (if you use all purpose flour add 1 teaspoon of sodium bicarb)

2 teaspoons vanilla

4 tablespoons cocoa

1 teaspoon Sodium Bicarbonate

flaked almonds - optional - for the top

In a large bowl mix all liquid ingredients, add mashed bananas, then sift dry ingredients and fold into mixture. Pour all into a loaf tin, sprinkle almonds over the top if you wish and bake for 45 to 50 minutes at 180 degrees C or 350 degrees F.

Love Brannie

MY QUILTING LIFE: EXPLOITS OF A QUILTY CAT

Ahhhhhhhhhhhhhh....! That's me, finally being able to relax after the visit by the Little People. They are such **busy** Little People!

They run and scream and wouldn't stop chasing me. When they would sit on the mat and play with stuff which looked very interesting, I would come out and sit on the mat nearby to watch, but then someone would see me and it was on again.

"Look, there's Brannie! Come on Brannie. Come on. Oh, she's gone under the bed."

After a bit they would forget about me and get on with interesting things and I could come out again to see what they were up to. But the next thing it was, "Look Brannie's on the chair under the table! You go that way and I'll go under and... Ohhh. Now she's gone under the couch."

I hardly slept for a week! They did go to bed earlier than me. I was able to get some quality "knee time" then.

It's pretty full-on having Little People visit. My Dad didn't get much time out in the shed and Mum certainly didn't get any quilting done.

She's since finished a wall hanging for the Littlies to play with though. It's got lots of dangly bits on it, so I have been able to help there. It's got ME on it too!

Mum took ages putting it together. She had it all in bits on the floor. I really stirred her up when I ran through it a couple of times! Boy, was she loud!

MY QUILTING LIFE: EXPLOITS OF A QUILTY CAT

It was quiet when the L/P's went home though. They were certainly very interesting. They even played with MY toys - threw my plastic rings and paper balls around. I didn't know what they were going to do next. Kept me on my toes, I can tell you!

We're having cooler weather now; I'm looking for a knee at every opportunity. Mum and Dad have started wearing long fluffy pants at night when they sit and watch the picture thing. Knees are really cosy then.

Must go - dinner's just arrived.

Love Brannie

MY QUILTING LIFE: EXPLOITS OF A QUILTY CAT

This morning my 'Quilty' Mum said she was going to die.
I was, naturally, quite concerned at first and I made the right sort of noises, but she seems all right to me.

I've kept my eye on her all day, just in case (actually, I did have a bit of a nap on the big chair for quite a while), but she has just been poking around as usual and I see no cause for alarm.

She got some pale fabric, twisted it all up and put rubber bands on it until it looked like a big messy knot.

Mum then went out to the garden and came back with an armful of green herbs. I think she called it "parcel" or something.

She shoved it all - material and parcel - into a big pot and started to cook it!! Smells awful!

I can't imagine what it will all taste like when she's finished! I hope she doesn't think **I'm** eating any for dinner!

Speaking of which, I might have to stir her up shortly. I've asked politely, smooched a bit, played with the string on the door knob beside her and then jumped up to the cutting place and walked across what she's doing.

Sometimes she just doesn't take the hint.

MY QUILTING LIFE: EXPLOITS OF A QUILTY CAT

I'd hate her to die on me before she gave me some meat!

She's just muttered, "It's not working anyway. Maybe it only works to make green wool". (I can't imagine wool would taste any better.)

She's heading for the cold cupboard. Great! It must be meat for dinner. When do we want it? **Naow!**

Love Brannie

MY QUILTING LIFE: EXPLOITS OF A QUILTY CAT

I was sitting on Mum's knee helping her with some hand sewing the other day.
She said, "You're a great help to me when I use light coloured thread. I can see it clearly against your dark brown fur when I thread the needle." I wriggled a bit and tried not to smirk. I continued to doze.

After a while, she said, "When we were away yesterday, I think you jumped up onto the sideboard, walked to the other end, then sat and looked around the room."

I opened my eyes real wide, but didn't move another muscle. **How did she know??** Is she somehow watching me when they're not here? Sounds like Big Mother to me. I'll have to give that a lot of thought. I might sleep on it. Apparently it is something to do with dust.

I got into a little bit of strife this morning. Dad brought in stuff from the garden and Mum said she would freeze it.

She was standing in the food room at the bench, going "Pop", then "rattle, rattle, rattle" into a dish. It got too much for me so I walked around to have a look and enquire what was going on.

Just as I arrived, she dropped a pea which bounced and rolled and, of course, I was onto it in a flash. What fun! Mum screeched, "Not under the fridge!!" just as I hit it......

Dad came in to find us both with heads on the floor and tails in the air trying to see where it had gone.

MY QUILTING LIFE: EXPLOITS OF A QUILTY CAT

I couldn't see what the problem was and asked for another one to play with, but she wasn't having any of it. Shortest game in history.

I'm going for a nap.

Love Brannie,

MY QUILTING LIFE: EXPLOITS OF A QUILTY CAT

"What's in a name?" I ask myself. They call me so many different things.

Do all you other 'Quilty' cats have lots of names, or is it just me?

"Hey, Funny Face. What are you up to?" Mum will say when I stroll by. "There's a Catty Poodle waiting for us!" she'll sing out when they come back from shopping.

My Dad is a bit more direct. "Hey You. Cat! Leave my shoes alone!" he'll yell. (He has one special pair of shoes he hides in the cupboard. The stringy bits are very chewable, so I have to be quick and quiet.)

Sometimes he'll shout "B.B." at me. That comes from him calling me Brownie Britches or Brownie Bu...er...Bottom.

I jumped up into the shelves with soft stuff the other day when Mum slid open the door to put towels away. She saw me unfortunately, held the door open and shouted "Out! Out damned Spot. Out I say!"

I raced up to the front room. Why did she call me Spot?? I'm almost sure I heard her mutter "...or get thee to a Cattery" as I flashed past.

I do actually have a few stray white hairs here or there, but you wouldn't call them spots. I have a birthday next week. I'm going to be a Big Girl Ten!

MY QUILTING LIFE: EXPLOITS OF A QUILTY CAT

Mum says I've passed her, now. I don't know how she worked that out. Ten sounds good to me - that's both whole front paws!

I can add up. It's Mum that has trouble. She is standing in front of the cutting table now saying..."4½ inch squares...then 3 7/8 inch.....cross cut twice...."

I know that when she really wants me to come to see something out the window she calls "Brannie!" loudly and then I run like mad because it's often a bird or rabbit really close and I like to see them.

'Quilty' Mums are funny aren't they? It doesn't really matter what they call us 'Quilty' cats, as long as they find us helpful.

Love Brannie

MY QUILTING LIFE: EXPLOITS OF A QUILTY CAT

I can't stop purring. Can you hear me? My 'Quilty' Mum says I have the loudest purr she knows!

I'm purring because she went away for ages and has now come back! Yay! She doesn't get to sit down for more than two ticks before I am on her knee again, purring. Why she wanted to go off to look at more quilts, I can't imagine, but away she went and came back talking funny.

"Hi Y'all!" she yelled at me. I looked around. There was only me here. Who was she talking to?

"Y'all look mahty fahn t'me" she went on. Where had this woman been?? Next she produced a big hat for my Dad; he's getting around looking like a Texan Cowboy now.

I don't know how long it will take her to return to normal. I'll just keep purring and try to help her with all these new quilts she wants to make. I don't know why she came back with more fabric. I thought she had enough here. Any ideas, 'Quilty' cats?

I had to look after my Dad while there were only two of us here. I helped him do computer stuff, I yelled out to him when he went over to the shed - ("Are you all right naowww?) - and I slept on top of him at night so he wouldn't be lonely or frightened of the Funder.

I did hear him on the phone-thing saying, "Oh, She's OK. She just won't leave me alone!" I'm not really sure who he was talking about there. I knew I was a great help though.

MY QUILTING LIFE: EXPLOITS OF A QUILTY CAT

Anyway my 'Quilty' Mum is home again. I'm purring, she's sewing and drawing more quilts, I'm still purring......but hang on. I am just going to hide under the bed for a bit. I can hear her getting out the Big Sucky Snake. I'm out of here until she stops that vacuum-y noise. It's dangerous and a girl can't hear herself purr with all that racket!

Love Brannie

~~~~~~~~~~~

You can read more of Brannie's Exploits in our Premium Online Quilt Magazine each month.

Go to www.OnlineQuiltMagazine.com to Subscribe.

~~~~~~~~~~~

Printed in Great Britain
by Amazon